EXCEPTIONAL
BEING THE EXCEPTION TO THE RULE

CASSIUS F. BUTTS
FOREWORD BY DR. LOUIS B. LYNN

EXCEPTIONAL

Being the Exception to the Rule

ISBN 978-1-949027-82-2

Cassius F. Butts info@cassiusbutts.com

Photo Credit: Eric Sun | ericsunphotography.com

Attorney Anthony L. Axam

Printed in the United States of America

Published by: Cassius F. Butts

www.CassiusButts.com

To my late father, Courlandt A. Butts, Sr., I hope I made you proud! My dearest Mother Barbara Ann Butts, thank you for first instilling God in your life which has blessed my life. My older brother Courtlandt, thank you for being a great brother of integrity and believing in me.

FOREWORD

by

DR. LOUIS B. LYNN

Though he is relatively young and in the mid-career phase of life, Cassius Butts has filled many important roles. Professionally, he has held positions that include bank president, federal government agency head, college professor, corporate executive, and serial entrepreneur. In addition to these various paying jobs, Cassius has distinguished himself as a civic leader, a community activist, a social activist leader, a political advisor, a fraternity leader, and a college trustee. I point out these areas of acumen only to highlight the heart and soul of Cassius Butts, i.e., "the man in the mirror."

My association and friendship with Cassius began as a business relationship in which he was my advisor and advocate. Cassius projected confidence while unabashedly displaying many godly and faith-based characteristics. As a man of faith, I watched him make godly decisions. Cassius is an optimist by choice. He is not a conformer but a visionary who seeks to reform certain aspects of the business arena to afford opportunities for under-served potential business people. He also has the skill of reconciling opposing viewpoints. As I got to know Cassius as a man of faith in the marketplace, I utilized my twenty-plus years as his senior to become one of his mentors. He recognizes and respects the experiences and wisdom of older folks as valuable contributors to his overall life journey. Likewise, he acknowledges that affluence, position, power, and success are seldom friends of faith and prayer.

To be EXCEPTIONAL means to be ready. A survey of Cassius's academic and business resume points to his preparedness. To be EXCEPTIONAL requires obedience and movement, which lead to success and blessings. The tariff for blessings is movement, and movement comes at a cost. As evidenced by his academic preparation, Cassius has spent considerable time getting the knowledge required of the READY. In addition to formal education, Cassius takes advantage of spending time and sitting under the tutelage of wise folks like Ambassador Andrew Young, former Atlanta Mayor Maynard Jackson, and some God-fearing men and women like me. Cassius has always had access to the kings of his culture, including state governors and even U.S. presidents. He has also had the ear of numerous captains of industry. Cassius was made READY because the journey is sometimes painful, often contentious, and potentially divisive. At this stage of his career, he accepts and expects that the journey to readiness never ends. It is apparent that early in life, Cassius was taught that "the future belongs to those who are prepared."

In this book, Cassius candidly shares heartfelt stories about his journey in the business world, from student to business executive to civil servant to entrepreneur. More importantly, as a man of faith, he gives an account of his life that demonstrates how it is possible to have a successful career that includes experience, expertise, and faith. The book highlights faith as an ever-present attribute of Cassius as he has filled different roles in the various seasons of his life, and he shares stories of how to battle encumbrances and stumbling blocks. Throughout the book, Cassius points out how faith, hard work, mentoring, performance, honesty, and justice are foundational to being a servant leader in the marketplace. Cassius even points out how "wilderness periods" can serve as incubators to "make ready" future servant leaders.

By the end of the book, the reader will understand that every season of one's life is poignant. While serving as the U.S. Small Business Administration (SBA) regional administrator, Cassius managed over $30 billion in loans to small business owners. During his tenure, the SBA worked with many small businesses to help them generate profits and create value in the marketplace. He made sure every business owner he worked with learned from others' failures, and he encouraged them by helping them model others' successes.

Using principles like this, Cassius has been able to provide a template for starting and growing a business. Cassius has had the privilege of working with and learning from entrepreneurs who were sure of where they were going and resolutely galloped in that direction with an unshakable conviction. And, he has also worked with business owners who were not so sure of their paths and ambled or drifted with varying degrees of care or attention to their business. As their advocate and enabler, Cassius has often instilled in the wavering business owner the belief that if an enterprise is worthwhile, it is deserving of one's best effort.

Through this book, Cassius is sharing some of those same lessons with you, and you'll get the benefit of learning to use these lessons to navigate your own path to success, whether you are a business owner or career professional.

Cassius' approach has helped several discouraged, disappointed, and doubting business owners. The faith-based message in the book emphasizes the benefits of absenting oneself from non-edifying commotion and diversions. His style has been to tell and show a startup business, not to confuse activity with progress. As SBA regional administrator, Cassius projected a spirit of support that telegraphed "GODSPEED" to those he advised and mentored. GODSPEED is a wish for the welfare of a person starting on a journey or venture. In the book, he illustrates that "to finish first, you have to first finish."

This book, *Exceptional*, has the features of an autobiography. Still, it is laced with many circumstances where Cassius and others in his life find and follow a faith-based roadmap to success. As a servant leader, Cassius is on a journey that shows his occupation is more than a means of earning money. His life journey illustrates how service to humanity exemplifies his labor and himself. In professional, civic, and social circles, Cassius has the unique skill of turning his personal opinions into convictions for himself and others. Throughout the book, some stories confirm that our deeds declare the passion and the bias of our hearts.

As a legitimate baby boomer, I sometimes riled Generation X (Gen X) audiences when I expressed concern to my peers about passing the torch to this Gen X crowd. Gen Xers like Cassius give us baby boomers hope and encouragement. Gen X leaders like Cassius recognize that the world beckons them to perform because their value to the world is based on their performance. From the outside looking in, watching Gen Xers find paths to success is refreshing. Successful business leaders across generations often show that their faith determines their moral compasses. Servant leaders often prove that faith is never a leap into the darkness. Their response to circumstances highlights that faith is based on the past. I now celebrate those Gen Xers who have recognized that there is no shortcut to the top and accept that hard work, honesty, and faith have a place in the marketplace. Gen X and millennial men and women like Cassius have figured out how to keep the faith as a constant companion. It is rewarding to see how caution, wise counsel, life callings, circumstances, and confirmations serve them well. Cassius accepts that leaders are sometimes burden bearers who are forced to show courage when making decisions. It's refreshing that they assume they must "stand in the gap" without fear. Employed courage authenticates faith. Each season of Cassius' life has been a new "finest hour."

Throughout the book, Cassius writes about several circumstances that demonstrate there are no inconsequential times in your life. This book illustrates that present obedience assures future BLESSINGS. These incidents show that circumstances, occasions, and associations that appear random and disconnected ARE NOT! The book promotes the benefits of living and working with intentionality. A faith-based and purpose-driven life always leads to success.

Exceptional specifically address particular life and faith experiences that make this a down-to-earth "good read." Overall, this book provides a candid and heartfelt overview of a faith-guided journey to success.

TABLE OF CONTENTS

CHAPTER 1

FINDING YOUR PASSION

Lessons from Morehouse College, Muhammad Ali and Dr. Rustin Lewis

Finding your passion is one of the fundamental steps you must take in identifying your purpose in life. Passion is finding that itch in your life—that desire to take an extra step in fulfilling the goals that lead you to your destiny.

People often speak about a fire that burns deep within their hearts, and they define that fire as passion. That fire that fuels us to make certain decisions that ultimately impact our lives and those of our family, co-workers, and friends. It is a fire you cannot describe to the non-dreamer. Yet it is an ever-present flame burning in those individuals who dream. The dreamer knows that

> **The dreamer knows that they are created for something special.**

they are created for something special, something unique to them. A holy grail that spurs them on the inside into constructing outward actions.

Finding your passion will ignite the confidence that you can achieve almost anything you want to in this life. It may require changing to a different profession, starting a new business, or even reaching for a recent achievement or goal lingering in your heart for years. Passion will enable you to face the ups and downs of life's challenges, identify the benchmarks needed for the development of your dream, and, most importantly, make it to the finish line.

SELF-ACTUALIZATION

There is a concept in psychology called **self-actualization**, which simply means, *to fulfill one's potential*. It is at the center of understanding the purpose of our lives. I remember my early days at the historic institution on the red clay hill in Atlanta, Georgia—Morehouse College. I have many fond memories of sitting under the instruction of Dr. Duane Jackson, the psychology department chair. He introduced many other students and me to this concept of self-actualization, which strengthened our fortitude and propelled us into leadership positions in a wide array of business, faith, and government positions.

Little did I know that my fellow alums would become some of our country's most influential citizens. Some of the students who were there during my matriculation are today's societal influences, such as pastors like Dr. Otis Moss III ('92), pastor of Chicago's Trinity United Church of Christ, Dr. Raphael Warnock ('91), Georgia Senator and senior pastor of the historic Ebenezer Baptist Church, and Dr. Jamal Bryant ('94), senior pastor of New Birth Missionary Baptist Church in DeKalb County, Georgia. Morehouse graduates have also become accomplished medical physicians, like Dr. Roger Morales ('92), CEO of Excellent Pediatrics, and Dr. Kevin Woods ('99), Head Gastroenterologist with Cancer Treatment Centers of America. Not only am I proud to know that these esteemed men are positive influencers in our society, but I am also proud to call them my very good friends.

My graduating class is affectionately known as "The Legendary Class of '94." It includes students who were destined to become historic alums. Verdun Perry, Global Head of Blackstone Strategic Partners, Euclid Walker, CGI Managing Director and Partner (who recently acquired the Trump Hotel in Washington, D.C.), and Nima Warfield, Morehouse

College's first Rhode Scholar. Our class exemplifies what is known as the "Morehouse Mystic."

Morehouse students continue to live by the model of one of our most notable alums, Howard Thurman, Class of 1923. He was known for saying, "Over the heads of her students, Morehouse holds a crown that she challenges them to grow tall enough to wear."

Hence, self-actualization is a term that became very real in my life and the lives of so many other Morehouse students. As the term implies, our inner selves become aware of being on a journey to discover why we are here. We ask questions such as "Why do I exist?" and "What can I achieve in this lifetime?" On the pathway to self-actualization, we identify who we are and how we develop our strengths and gifts; we even recognize our weaknesses. If we are true to our search for purpose, we will find our passion on that journey.

A SUITABLE MARRIAGE

Passion and self-actualization go hand in hand in one's search for purpose. What hinders many people is the daunting task of considering the steps needed to get to that optimal place where self-actualization and passion marry. Much maturing is required before we initiate the effort to obtain these two partners. For others, it takes a catastrophe that jars the mind into recognizing that taking a risk to find yourself is better than not trying. For me, it was a catastrophic event that spurred me into action.

Taking a risk to find yourself is better than not trying.

AN ICY BEGINNING

I was born in Philadelphia, Pennsylvania, in the 1970s, when our country sought to make the American Dream a reality for all. I was fortunate to have both parents, Courtlandt A. Butts, Sr., and Barbara Ann Butts, as well as my brother, Courtlandt A. Butts, Jr., who all played a significant part in my growth and development.

My brother excelled at academics, even skipping grades in elementary school. As a result, my father nicknamed him

"The Professor." My physical outlet was sports, and I loved the competition that went along with it. In addition, my brother and I engaged in a wide array of activities, one of which I credit to my mother—learning the art of entrepreneurship.

My brother and I wanted a Star Wars bedding ensemble and all the action figures that were part of the movie. These were the most coveted action figures during my childhood. So we asked our mother for the money to buy the set, and she kindly replied, "How about you earn enough money to buy your own?" It was summer, and one of our pastimes was making frozen fruit drinks, better known as "icy cups." Had I known then what I know now, we could have copyrighted that name and made a fortune!

Our mother suggested we sell icy cups to our friends for 25 cents each. That's right, only 25 cents! So my brother and I began to sell the icy cups, and our first business was born. One day, I came home and asked my mother if I could have a larger cup and sell the icy cups for 50 cents each. She replied, "Now you are thinking like a businessman." By the end of the summer, we had sold so many icy cups that we had enough money to pay for the entire set of action figures, the complete bedding ensemble, *and* the matching window treatments. It was my first taste of entrepreneurship, and I loved it! Over the years, my brother, friends, and I established a car washing, landscaping, and clothing business. We also made it a point to join business programs that included the youth, such as the Future Business Leaders of America, Junior Achievement, and the Young Men of Tomorrow.

A NIGHTMARE THAT LED TO PURPOSE

Later, my family moved to Orlando, Florida, where my father accepted a position as an engineer with Martin Marietta Aerospace. I did not realize at the time the significance that this type of opportunity had for my family. Best of all, my brother and I could spend every summer in Philadelphia with our grandparents, which afforded us the best of both worlds. It was great spending time with other family members.

My graduation from high school provided a memory that I will never forget. My grandparents came to our home in Orlando to attend my graduation. Most people look upon their graduation with fond memories of the family love and support they receive for the recognition of their achievement. However, the day before I graduated, my maternal grandmother, Ednonia Beeks, asked a favor of me. She was raised in South Carolina, where she married my grandfather, Daniel Beeks, Sr. My grandmother was known as an excellent cook and planned on cooking breakfast, lunch, and dinner for the family that day. However, she needed some items from the grocery store, and I volunteered to pick them up.

I quickly grabbed my mother's car keys and dashed out of the house. In the early summer months, Orlando was known to have sudden bursts of rain called sun-showers. I remember that day, the sun was hitting the pavement, and I could see the steam from the rain rising from the concrete. My mother, an educator and entrepreneur, had established a family daycare. That day, she was at the front door with one of her clients and her daughter. Like on most days, the neighborhood was full of pedestrians and children riding bicycles. But, unbeknownst to me, the daughter of one of my mother's friends was playing in our driveway. She was only three years old.

The temperature was so warm that day as I got in the car that I rolled down the window and started the engine. I looked in the rear-view mirror as I hastily shifted the car into reverse. My desire to make a fast trip to the store motivated me to push the pedal faster than usual. Suddenly, I heard a huge thump and felt the back left side of the car lift over what I thought was a huge rock. I slammed on the brakes and immediately I heard screams from the people in the front yard. I placed the car in park and exited to investigate what had happened. It was my worst nightmare. I saw that I had hit the toddler who, just a moment before, had been playing in our front yard.

You can only imagine what was going through my head when this accident occurred. I was supposed to be celebrating my most outstanding achievement up to that point, and all that was going through my mind were questions: "Did I kill her?" "Was there anyone else hurt?" "What do I do now?" Within seconds, I scooped her up in my arms and started praying. I cried, "O God, please let her be okay." The child gasped for air and appeared motionless. Suddenly she released a loud, piercing scream, and her mother ran over and grabbed her from my arms.

By this time, the ambulance had arrived. The local authorities interviewed me and everyone else at the scene. I was suffering from an internal pain that I would not wish on anyone. The medical team examined the little girl and found that, miraculously, she sustained only a broken arm. I could only classify this as a miracle! One of the witnesses recounted that they could not understand how the toddler had survived the accident. Another witness claimed she had seen the car hit the child but could not explain how the vehicle had risen high enough to keep the child from significant injuries. Only a higher entity could have protected this child and spared everyone the suffering that something more serious would have caused.

It was then I realized that not only did that little girl have a purpose in this world, but so did I. If you are fortunate to find out who you are at an early age, it can be helpful on your journey. I was lucky to realize at this time that both of us, the little toddler and myself, had a higher purpose in this world and that it was my job to find and fulfill my purpose. I realized how precious life is, which became ingrained in me as I understood that purpose was something you had to seek. This unfortunate situation enabled me to become more mindful of my surroundings. It helped me to make better decisions,

I understood that purpose was something you had to seek.

personally and professionally. I found a passion for serving people, even in my pursuit of finding myself, which made me a better human being.

COMPETITION AT ITS BEST

Another memorable moment came at a time in my life when I discovered my self-esteem. I am not an advocate for social competition, but I enjoy competing against myself in life's journey, particularly in sports. I have played organized sports such as boxing, track, and especially football since I was a young kid. To this day, I compete in weekly pick-up basketball games at the YMCA. I credit those competitive activities for helping me to succeed in my professional life. My parents allowed my brother and me to play Pop Warner football in elementary school. I also played football in junior high and high school at Edgewater H.S. in Orlando, Florida. I played the position of running back.

Recently, I had a chance to meet one of the greatest running backs in NFL history, Emmitt Smith. He played for Escambia H.S. in Pensacola, Florida. I told Emmitt I looked up to him, as did many others in Florida during that time. Studying athletes who made a name for themselves was one of my pastimes. It stemmed from listening to stories about my grandfather, Daniel Beeks, Sr., who was a professional boxer while serving in the Army and won the Army Championship Boxing tournament. He once even sparred with the legendary Joe Louis.

Having these sports legends in my life motivated me to pursue competitive sports. I learned a lot, primarily how to deal with losing. I worked hard and had great opportunities. I even practiced with the greatest of all time, Muhammad

Ali, who gave me tips on "using my jab" to keep my opponent from hitting me. I received a lot of positive encouragement in my formative years, which built my confidence and fueled my passion. You learn a lot after being knocked down several times. You begin to understand that picking yourself up amidst the battle is necessary. I saw that hard knocks helped me build character, revealing what was inside me—who I was, my true self.

Hard knocks helped me build character.

There are many people like me for whom these types of experiences are what it takes to get to that next level of maturity required for leadership. Sometimes we must go through challenges that will be as tough as nails. Yet, we must strive to obtain and possess a positive mindset. And, when you don't have people around you to keep you positive, sometimes, the motivator must be the person in the mirror.

TURNING PASSION INTO A PLAN

What we are passionate about is our purpose, and our purpose becomes our plan. This notion is based on what I learned early in graduate school. As we open our minds to discovering our purpose, we learn what we are passionate about. As you pursue your passion, you truly learn who you are, what you're made of, and how you can contribute to society and fulfill those dreams within yourself. Finding your true self and purpose is what makes the world go around.

Even mature people can find that they are not in a place to figure out this thing called life. We are all seeking to understand why we are here on this earth. Many people, perhaps even you, desire to know what their contribution to society should be. What wakes you up every day? Realizing what motivates you to get up every day and travel on the road of productivity is the beginning to identifying your purpose. You may not have it all figured out at once, and all days will not be the same. Some days will be better than others. Life is about how we respond to challenges, situations, and predicaments.

Life is about how we respond to challenges, situations, and predicaments.

Your purpose may begin with a desire to be better within your households first. It could be a desire to be a better executive or role model. It could be a desire to be a better educator, mentor, or family member. It could be a desire to be a better and more effective policymaker or even a better human being. Dr. Rustin Lewis, author and accomplished nonprofit executive, has been a close friend of mine for over 25 years. Through avid conversations over the years, I credit him for often helping me see life's more significant possibilities. Whatever your passion is, when you put time and effort into molding and shaping your life around it, you will find yourself in a better place. That is when you begin to find harmony in your life. That is true for the young and the seasoned alike.

What are you passionate about?
How are you using your passion to fuel your purpose?

CHAPTER 2

CHECKING YOUR EGO

Lessons from Secretary of State Condoleezza Rice's speech to my presidential management fellow class and my U.S. Small Business Administration appointment by President Barack Obama

When we walk into a room, one of the first things we do is observe who and what is in it. We assess those we see in the room. It could be a boardroom, a training room, or an office building. We look to see who is there and whether we can find a familiar face. Typically, we also look to see if there is anyone we can connect with, anyone to make us feel comfortable. That is not unusual. It is a normal human reaction. We want to find someone to connect with, and we consciously or unconsciously determine who will be a friend and who might be a foe. When we walk into a room to display true success, no matter what position we are in, it behooves us to check our egos at the door before we walk through.

It behooves us to check our egos at the door before we walk through.

It may not be the easiest or simplest thing to do. However, being an open vessel to those you are coming to share with and those looking to absorb the wisdom you have to offer will be best received if you check your ego at the door. We must understand that no matter who we are, our title, or where we are, we all have egos. They are that fragile part of our confidence. During my time as a presidential management fellow during the George W. Bush administration, Secretary of State Condoleezza Rice entered the room to give remarks to our group of fellows. Before she walked in, everyone was talking and sharing stories of the things they were experiencing. Secretary Rice approached the microphone, paused without saying a word, and then smiled at the audience. She recognized that we were just as excited to hear her give remarks as she was to provide them. You could have heard a pin drop. Then she gave a resounding speech that inspired all of us. There were many other dignitaries and officials in the room. Many of them commanded the same respect as Secretary Rice. While in deep conversations with other attendees, I noticed that they quickly checked their egos and gave her the attention she had earned. I also remember how honored I felt to be among many people passionate about government. Secretary Rice reminded us that our commitment to public service is essential to the well-being of our country.

I learned a lot that day. First, I noticed that you must do something with your ego to make space to glean from the experiences others will encounter. When we do not check our egos and walk into a room full of ourselves, people who may try to interact with us will miss the opportunity to give or even receive wisdom because we don't have enough space left in our hearts. And there needs to be more space because there is too much ego in the way.

Sometimes the ego is even a misrepresentation of the individual. In many instances, it can be a cover-up for pride or evidence of a lack of self-confidence that presents itself as a strong ego. In most cases, it is a feeling of being uncertain about oneself that inhibits character development. We become insecure with who we are, making us afraid of our success. We become hesitant before a big crowd or around people with whom we are not familiar. One thing is sure: people fear the unknown, and sometimes that means even the unknown of potential triumphs and successes. Conversely, if there is an expectation that the value we as individuals bring will lend itself to the good of those we are addressing in the room, we will leave gratified, and so will they. Setting our bar of expectations, we recognize that we can pack our egos in our back pockets and keep walking toward success, always remembering that no matter what happens, we possess all we need to reach our goals.

REAL LEADERS KNOW IT

When we do not follow this pattern of checking our egos, our egos can limit us. And when that happens, we may not make sound decisions. Our confidence deflates, and ultimately, we cannot deliver what we are expected to share. Ego can put us in a place where we have difficulty pursuing those we need to communicate with or who have something to impart. However, if we put that ego away, it can change the trajectory of our lives, opening the door for wonderful interactions with others. Successful people recognize that they don't have to prove their worth; they walk in it.

Successful people recognize that they don't have to prove their worth; they walk in it.

It begins with us knowing our minds. Embracing a competitive mindset helps us achieve confidence. A competitive attitude does not necessarily mean competing with other people, places, or things in front of us. Instead, adopt the mindset that you are your own competition. When we compete with ourselves, we

When we compete with ourselves, we become better people.

become better people. This thinking creates better character within and also reveals it without. Being exceptional means adopting a standard of excellence such as this to bring about success.

During my time at the U.S. Small Business Administration (SBA), I was appointed by President Obama to lead, inspire, and provide access to capital in the millions to small businesses and entrepreneurs. I was proud to be the first African American in that position within Region Four. I didn't realize this until one of Atlanta's most prominent entrepreneurs, Mack Wilbourn, informed me of that historical fact. Mack was a close friend of my mentor, Maynard Jackson, the former Mayor of Atlanta. Mack currently owns the most successful Popeyes© franchises in the world. After receiving guidance from Mack, I realized that the success of our agency depended upon a team effort to achieve success. Julius Hollis, another person from whom I received guidance, founded Air Atlanta and his late brother Michael. He and Mack often remind me to recognize those who created these business pathways for individuals like me. I never gave a speech, addressed dignitaries, or highlighted achievements without first speaking about the mission of our department and the people we served. This practice of putting others first gave me my rhythm in that role. I understood that I had to let our internal and external advocates know that the agency's

> **This practice of putting others first gave me my rhythm.**

lifeblood rested upon those who needed this service most— the people we served. I modeled this every time that I spoke.

Relationships are essential. I often would have these conversations with a close friend who could actually relate to the trials and tribulations on the road to achieving my goals. Christopher Upperman was also a presidential appointed official who served with me during the Obama Administration. He walks with purpose and always carry a sense of humility on his shoulder. There were many instances in which Christopher had to check his own ego to support others in their professional endeavors. It is not always easy. However, once you put your ego in perspective, you gain a wealth of experience and knowledge unintentionally. I believe those experiences paved new experiences for him. Chris is now Head of Governance and Partnerships for Facebook/Meta. I am deeply proud of his accomplishments and still to this day learn from his drive and determination to achieve success.

While reading this, ask yourself these questions: Do you encourage those you lead? Are you convinced you can be confident yet respectful to those around you? People are attracted to those who exhibit humility. It is not always an easy practice, but it is worth it. I am often asked how I can speak to such large groups of people and be relaxed. Some of my peers have wondered if I am afraid or intimidated. I always respond that I feel the same gut-twisting emotions, face the same challenges as they do, and have the same butterfly feeling in my stomach. I have just learned that in one of my back pockets is my bar of excellence and that it is with me; I own it. And if I own it, no matter what happens when I walk onto or off the stage, I'm walking with my own excellence. If I remember that I have that bar, I have the confidence to do the job. The great thing about this concept is that you can utilize your bar of excellence as often as you need to—it never gets old.

REAL LEADERSHIP GROWS LEADERS

Another principle of leadership is that a true leader's success is contagious. CEOs and other executives led to the development of more leaders. I come from a school of thought that says a captain is only as good as their crew. Therefore, it is necessary to take all steps to move the entire organization forward, even if it means delivering a message your team may not want to hear. True leadership means you make tough decisions that ensure the deliverables are on time and under budget. I once

True leadership means you make tough decisions.

learned an important truth: "While you are leading, you are doing so with a sense of conviction and assurance that you believe in your team, that they can do it!"

In a class of his own, President Barack Obama exhibited an exceptional leadership style that empowered his appointed officials to carry out their responsibilities using their best qualities to obtain success. He believed those respective appointees would work best using their unique techniques. Therefore, he gave them the freedom to do their job, and success followed throughout his administration. The slogan "Yes, we can" flowed through his appointed team. He showed that he believed in the people he set to carry out the mission of public service. These are the marks of a good leader: exuding confidence, leaving a checked ego at the door, having a CEO mindset, and trusting your team always to make the right decision as long as transparency, integrity, and humility are part of the equation. People will know that you are in leadership for a reason.

There will be tough days when you as the leader must bear huge amounts of responsibility, but when you operate with a standard of excellence, you realize that this can happen, and you know you can handle it. People are looking to see how you weather the storms that often come about unexpectedly. Do you continue to push forward, making tough decisions with humility? I saw this kind of leadership with the late Arizona senator, John McCain. Senator McCain was known for mentoring junior senators from both sides of the aisle (Republicans and Democrats). Senator McCain had close relationships with many of the world's famous from all walks of life. Some of those relationships were surprising, like the one he had with Muhammad Ali. Their relationship was something that most people would not think possible—two unlikely allies. It was just another example of how you can't judge a book by its cover. Have you ever assumed that certain people would never get along or work well together? Sometimes that prejudgment causes us to ignore

People are looking to see how you weather the storms.

the possibility that even though two people may seem diabolically opposed, they might actually become best friends. Well, that is what happened with Senator McCain and Muhammad Ali. It was not surprising that due to the work his family did with Muhammad Ali, Cindy McCain, Senator McCain's wife, received a lifetime achievement award from the Muhammad Ali Foundation in 2016.

Have you had a time when you should have checked your ego but didn't and perhaps missed a great opportunity?"

CHAPTER 3

BELIEVING IN YOURSELF

Lessons from T. Dallas Smith on having a seat at the table instead of being on the menu

Believing in yourself is one of the most important disciplines you must master before engaging in any personal or professional endeavor. Unfortunately, belief is something that is often underestimated and many times are taken for granted.

People tend to look for a connection or entity that empowers them or allows them to accomplish whatever obstacle they face. Before you believe in anything outside of yourself, you must believe in yourself.

> **Before you believe in anything outside of yourself, you must believe in yourself.**

You, as an individual, exist because you have a purpose. What you have to offer has value and meaning, so it stands to reason that others have meaning and purpose, too. If you start believing in yourself, you can conquer anything. It does not matter if you were a motherless or fatherless child or if you didn't have a mentor to guide you; no matter what barriers you faced, the moment you opened your eyes to this world, you were given a purpose. It's time for you to get into it and become a part of this game of life. Life cannot begin for you until you decide you are going to be a part of it. That is how important it is to participate. No matter what title anyone holds, no matter what social or economic place they come from, everyone is just as important as every other person—and yes, that means you, too!

Life cannot begin for you until you decide you are going to be a part of it.

OUR TEACHERS ARE EVERYWHERE

On my travels to my many engagements, I spend as much time speaking to the security guard at the door, the administrative assistant at the front office, or the cab driver who drove me to my destination as I talk to my designated audience. Each person holds the same value as a CEO. I find comfort and wisdom in spending time with those in administrative support roles, for I can learn from anyone. But, again, each person holds the same value as the person sitting next to them.

Once we realize the equal worth of all individuals, we can then accept that we are all part of the same system.

Once we realize the equal worth of all individuals, we can then accept that we are all part of the same system, and that system is called life. So, first, we believe in ourselves, and then we believe that we are part of something bigger than ourselves. I'm not asking you to pick a religion or a political party; I'm asking you to look in the mirror and realize that you are but one somebody among other somebodies! It's that simple.

You will note that I often refer to my upbringing to bring my perspective into balance. How we think helps project our futures. How frequently have you asked yourself, "Can I do this?" It is crucial to surround yourself with people who believe in you, no matter what kind of endeavor you pursue.

T. Dallas Smith founded a commercial real estate company (T. Dallas Smith & Company, Inc.) in the middle of the housing crisis, around 2008. He lost everything because of the market crash. He was asked in a recent interview, "Why would you start a company in the middle of chaos?" His answer was simple: "I believe in myself and what I was born to do." Today, as CEO, he has landed some of the country's most significant real estate transactions, and as his close friend, I consistently seek him out for advice.

Dallas and I often talk about the importance of relationships. Real estate mogul H. J. Russell had a saying that resonated with both of us: "If you don't have a seat at the table, you're probably on the menu."

> **"If you don't have a seat at the table, you're probably on the menu."**
>
> **– T. Dallas Smith**

You are who you are because you first believe in yourself. No matter your political affiliation or membership in social organizations, you are your first and biggest fan. Take a moment to reflect on that concept. *Do you truly see yourself as your biggest fan?*

If you don't remember anything else about these lessons for success, remember that all success begins with you believing in yourself first. If you can't readily accept this, look to family members, colleagues, and even co-workers you trust that may have seen you perform at your optimum level. Get the opinion of these people, for other people often see the greatness in you that you can't see within yourself.

Is there someone or something in your life that reminds you to believe in yourself?

CHAPTER 4

SETTING REALISTIC GOALS

Lessons on setting goals, accountability and partnerships

I remember a time a few years ago when I was walking up a flight of stairs. I had to pause and catch my breath when I reached the top of the stairs. After that, I was like, "Whoa, okay." It was near springtime, the perfect time to put some exercise in my life.

With that being said, I didn't expect to lose any specific number of pounds or be in tip-top shape the following week. Instead, I realized that I had to set realistic goals over a period of time. When you set realistic goals, you begin to build yourself up, and you encourage yourself. You also start to build confidence and a belief in your ability to complete your long-range goals by meeting your benchmarks one at a time. Once you begin to embark on the process, it enables you to make goal-setting a way of life.

When I ask clients to set realistic goals, I'm not asking them to set realistic goals to achieve a certain plateau and then stay there or walk away from it. Instead, I'm asking them to commit to changing their lifestyles. In essence, I'm asking them to implement a way of governing themselves so that it can be used for the rest of their lives.

You can attain the ultimate goal you desire to achieve. It could be weight loss or starting and growing a business; the process is the same. I stopped eating red meat and pork when I was twenty years old. People asked me if I had missed it. My ready response was always, "No, I don't." Why? Because there are specific health issues that run in my family. I decided that if I made specific health changes early, I could avoid certain ailments.

Others ask me how I'm doing with my regimen; how do I maintain a vibrant mindset? Although many roads lead to better health, I decided that every ten years of my life, I would cut something out of my diet that I felt was not good for me. That is a realistic goal. I made this decision because I know my body cannot break down food like it did when I was a teenager or even in my twenties. So I consciously cut certain things out and set realistic goals for myself, determining that I would not eat this or that group of foods anymore for the rest of my life.

Additionally, I took the time to prepare and get into that perspective. It began with changing my mindset and then changing my lifestyle and implementing positive habits. It not only pertains to a personal way of eating but also to business. As we have learned from our recent worldwide battle with COVID-19, we all must change how we obtain and consume foods, and those foods must be healthier. It is not an easy task, but living through this pandemic has forced us to make necessary changes, and some of those changes have had to become permanent.

Living through this pandemic has forced us to make permanent changes.

When I was in college, my roommate and I once talked about changing our lifestyles. A brand-new wonder product was out to help you lose weight. There was also a product out to help you gain weight. He was trying to gain weight during our college days. We were in a position where we couldn't buy certain foods like fruit or healthy foods that wouldn't damage our digestive systems. It was challenging to do because we could only purchase non-perishable foods. We were determined to eat a certain way, wanting fresh fruits and vegetables, but the foods we needed to eat could not be preserved in our dorm room. What we needed was a refrigerator!

INVESTMENT IN. SUCCESS OUT.

Now apply this to your business. The best thing you can do is invest in something that will allow you to have the things that will be productive for your business and keep it healthy. If you have the equivalent of something like a refrigerator to sustain you over time, your business will run more efficiently. On the other hand, if you can't invest in the proper equipment or human power and instead try to make do with things or people who are ill-equipped to do the job, you will see the results.

My dorm roommate and I became accountable to each other. We made sure that each of us stuck to our plan, even with its limitations, to the extent possible. Having someone that you are accountable to in business is vitally important. People who

Having someone that you are accountable to is vitally important.

go into business underestimate the value of partnerships and accountability, feeling they can solve any challenges they will face by themselves. That could be considered naïve, and we will discuss it further in another chapter.

What are the top 3 goals you want to accomplish in the next year? Three years? Who can you trust to keep you accountable?

CHAPTER 5

YOUR FAITH WILL NEVER FAIL YOU

Lessons in Prayer and Obedience

Faith is something that has been at the forefront of everything that I do. Whenever I face challenges or need inspiration, I always rely on something related to my faith to pull me through. I often acknowledge that my faith is the reason for any successes or positive results in my walk. We often face challenges and have to figure out our next steps. Have you ever been in a place where it's dark, where you were not sure what the next day would bring? Does your mind keep asking questions like What am I doing? Am I even making an impact? Am I essential in the scheme

> **My faith is the reason for any successes or positive results in my walk.**

of things? I ask myself these questions every day. It is not part of my conversation with others; it is the conversation I have with myself. I reflect on the results of my actions. What is happening with my career? Am I on the right track? Am I serving people, or am I just doing a job? Am I fulfilling my life calling, and have I kept to my faith?

I was worked in corporate America after I left More-house College and was trying to figure out what I wanted to do with my life. I wasn't sure at that point. So I began working for a financial institution through its management development program. During that time, a new community reinvestment policy was introduced within the federal financial banking system. It was a new policy to ensure equity and representation were disbursed among all communities. At that time, Oprah Winfrey produced a show in Forsyth County, Georgia, that addressed issues amongst minority and majority communities. I was sent there to be part of that representation. After fulfilling the assignment, I remember returning to my office that night and sitting at my desk. I checked the box on finishing a successful project. I remember asking, "Is this what my life will be about? Merely checking a box?"

Is this what my life will be about?

As I sat there that night, I prayed, "God, if this is not what you want me to do, what is it that you want me to do? I am not fulfilled. I am not happy. I don't feel as though I'm making a difference the way I want to make a difference." Almost immediately, a presence came to me, speaking to me the way I am. The presence in my mind said, "Leave." I remember searching my office for anyone who might still be there. The office was dark, with only one light on—the light at my desk. There was no one else there.

My conversation and prayer with myself continued. I thought I heard something say, "Leave." Immediately going back into prayer mode, I started asking the Lord, "What is it that you want from me? Tell me now; I want to be sure. I want to know what I'm supposed to do right now." Once again, I heard a presence say, "Leave."

A LEAP OF FAITH

Scripture tells us that **obedience is better than sacrifice**. So, what did I do? I did what most people would not do.

The next day, I went downtown and tendered my resignation letter. People honestly didn't understand

I did what most people would not do.

my actions. They told me of all the benefits of remaining on the job: "You have a great office. You have a great job. You're one of the few in the position to do what you are doing." I replied all to those who spoke, "I'm not happy." And so, I gave it up. I left my job and made some sound financial decisions to manage my immediate bills. I remember then going to see Anthony Lacy, my college roommate, and having him continue the drill I had received earlier:

"Man, what are you doing?" he asked. "You're supposed to be at work."

"I quit my job," I said.

"You did what?" he replied.

"Yeah."

"Why?" he asked

"I just wasn't happy."

And then he asked me something that I already knew deep down in my gut: "What enabled you to do that?"

"My faith," I said. "My faith is stronger than anything else in my life."

"My faith is stronger than anything else in my life."

I remember trying to figure out what I was going to do next. I didn't have a clue. I just knew that I was relying on my faith to guide me.

FAITH'S CHALLENGES AND REWARDS

What happened next? I remember going out to sell my compact discs (CDs). I had a vast collection of compact music discs—over 3,000. In the late '90s, you could sell or trade CDs. So, I sold mine to a music retail store.

Afterward, I went to buy some noodles, the kind you could heat up in a steam pot. While I was driving home, my car hit a huge pothole and had a blowout. As I changed the tire, it started raining. I broke down and started releasing all my emotions. I was at the end of my rope. I thought that I had done everything I was supposed to do to be successful and flourish in my career; I felt that by making a list of things, I would be satisfied and happy.

"God," I said, "is this what you want for me? I did what you told me to do. This place cannot be where I'm supposed to be currently in my life."

Again, a presence that told me, "Read my book of Job." I remember looking around; no one else was there. Now people will say, "Are you off your rocker? Are you one of those?" No, I'm just a regular guy, like everyone who believes in their faith. I read the book of Job, and it was a fascinating story. The next day I received a message. It was when pagers, not cell phones, were popular. I called the number back, and someone asked, "Are you, Mr. Butts?"

"Yes," I replied.

"We would like you to come to the City of Atlanta human resources department. We understand you are looking for an internship."

I could hardly contain my excitement. "Yes, I am. I graduated from Morehouse and am planning to attend graduate school, and I am looking for an internship."

"Okay, great," the person on the other end of the line said. "That's fine; you can begin on Monday."

"I haven't filled out any paperwork."

"Don't worry," he said. "You can fill it out when you get here."

Okay, I thought to myself. I asked, "Is there an opportunity to earn any money because I need to..."

Before I could finish my sentence, she said, "Well, I don't know. You must be important to someone because we'll start you off with a salary." The salary was about $32,000 at the time, which was a lot of money for me.

"Whoa, okay," I said.

I realized that I had given a speech as the class president of my graduate school at Clark Atlanta University School of Public Administration. My mentor, the former Mayor of Atlanta, Maynard Jackson—the giant he was—believed in me. I never asked him for anything, yet he opened a door for me. Was it him, or was it the answer to the questions I had asked God? As I thought about it, I couldn't help remembering how God said He would never leave or forsake us. And I began to know that God uses those vessels in our lives to bring us to the next place He has for us.

I started working as an intern in the city of Atlanta. I began to develop knowledge and skills in assisting small and mid-size businesses to obtain capital. My graduate exit paper was on the City of Atlanta's Equal Business Opportunity Program, which today has amassed over six billion dollars in airport and city support alone! I had an opportunity to help

minorities, women, and others excluded from business opportunities to live out their entrepreneurial dreams.

I was very proud of that accomplishment, and the best
news is that the program is still in existence today. That is
an example of where my faith helped me, and it is one that I
will never forget. Everything I have done up to this point has
been born out of my faith. Can you look back over your life
and recognize that someone was present to help you get out
of the dark places, something bigger than you? For me, it was
my faith.

Think of a time when you had to rely on your faith.

What did you learn from that experience?

CHAPTER 6

HUMOR CAN BE YOUR BIGGEST ASSET

Lessons from having the last name "Butts"... and why Dale Murphy says we are better when we laugh at ourselves

When I reflect on the events in my life, I always pause to smile and even find a way to laugh. Some of my favorite people in this life are comedians. In fact, at one point in my life, I daydreamed of dropping out of college to become a comedian. I never even told my family about that; I thought they would think I had lost it! Yet my brother and I grew up listening to Richard Pryor, Gene Wilder, Cedric the Entertainer, Seinfeld, and Steve Harvey, to name a few. We would also hear about Eddie Murphy and others like him, who took the hard times of this life and made fun of them. One of my fondest examples is the movie *Stir Crazy*, about two guys trying to make it in life who were accused of a crime they didn't commit. The comedy illustrates how they used their wits to escape situations and were eventually exonerated.

So, I grew up doing the same thing. I found something to laugh and smile about whenever there were hard times. Life can be tricky. It can be challenging. But humor can get you through those difficult times. Sharing your laughter can lighten loads of those around you and help them not take themselves or their situations so seriously. People will ask me when they see me laughing to myself, "What are you laughing at?" I will unashamedly answer them, "I'm thinking about a Richard Pryor joke, or when Gene Wilder said this, or when Amy Schumer or Eddie Murphy said such and such." It will then begin a conversation. Humor has become a door that has opened to opportunities to interact with the people around me.

Life has two sides. It can be great with everything going your way. On the flip side, life can also be a rat race in which troubles can bring you down, where you can find no humor in anything. I don't let life get me to that place. I must be able to laugh, even if life is laughing at me! I can't take things so seriously that I get down, that I get holed up in a place where I don't think I can accomplish what I'm trying to do. I look for the humorous side of a situation, and it brings me out of feeling down and helps me to look for the way out.

Humor is one of those keys that will unlock dark places and shine a little light onto whatever you are dealing with. And it's contagious. When people allow

Humor is one of those keys that will unlock dark places.

themselves the opportunity to laugh without embarrassment, it makes everyone feel better and more productive.

MAKING IT WORK FOR YOU

In a recent interview, I was asked if I had a personal story about something in my life that I did not find funny that I had to overcome. It wasn't hard to answer that, for something obvious that I was ribbed about was my last name, Butts. Growing up, I was the brunt of many jokes. The interviewer wanted to know how I handled it. It was not always an easy thing to do. My hesitancy to give my last name began in grade school when the kids would laugh when the teacher would say my name. I thought of ways to turn that into positive attention. That carried on into my professional life. Whenever I went to speak to a group of kids, I would ask the principal not to introduce me by my last name. I didn't want them to laugh at me. Eventually, I decided to use this to my advantage. I decided I wanted them to laugh at me so that I could laugh too! I finally figured out that if they were laughing and I was laughing, it would be easier to deliver my message.

Growing up, my grandmother sent me and my brother clothes, records, movies, and Philadelphia Eagles paraphernalia. There was one time when my grandmother sent us clothes. We were going to a racing competition at school, and we decided we would wear the new shorts she had sent. We took the clothes out of the delivery box and changed into the car on the day of the race. We had already determined that if we wore these new clothes, they would help us to run faster. We noticed how many runners wore sporty red shorts with track lines and how well they did. We figured if we wore sporty track shorts, we would also win the competitions.

On the way to the race, I put my shorts in the car. Running out of the car, I didn't realize until I got out that I was wearing my brother's shorts. They were much bigger than I needed, although my brother had a pair that fit him just fine. I had to hold the pants up as I raced to get to the starting line of the competition. It was a hundred-yard dash, and I was already running late; there was no time to change. The gun went off, and there was nothing to do but begin the race. The whole time I ran, the shorts fell, and I had to keep pulling them up. Finally, I just held onto them and ran as fast as possible. I ran so fast that I was able to come in second. My classmate Terry came in first. He was the star athlete in our class. He ribbed me, saying, "I came in first, and you came in second; you're slow!" Trying to play it off, I said, "Yeah, I came in second. The Butts man came in second while holding his shorts!" I used their jokes about my name myself. I continued, saying, "If I didn't have to hold up my shorts, I would have beat you." And everyone laughed. It became the joke of our class. After that, everyone started calling me the "Butts man." Even today, people who knew me then will say, "Hey, Butts, man!" I took what people did to make fun of me and turned it into something that people did in a friendly manner, all because I laughed myself. It was a lesson learned that has served me well.

There are times when humor becomes your best friend. I host a podcast called "The Winning Way by Cassius F. Butts." During Season 2, I interviewed Atlanta Braves Baseball Hall of Famer Dale Murphy. Dale and I are friends and business partners. He advised me in that interview not to take life too seriously; he reminded me that you miss out on life's greatest moments if you can't laugh at yourself. These are words that I will always treasure.

You miss out on life's greatest moments if you can't laugh at yourself.

Do you have a story or memory where you have laughed at yourself? Can you think of a time when you did something wild or unexpected, and you became the center of attention?

Have you ever turned what was a difficult situation around through humor?

CHAPTER 7

BUILDING A DYNASTY OUT OF AN INTERNSHIP

Lessons from volunteering and interning and how Atlanta Mayor, Maynard Jackson, and others inspired me to give in service to others

When I was growing up, teenagers found different artists that motivated them. I love music. I love everything from the Bee Gees, Tupac, Janet Jackson, and Baby Face to Outkast and Drake—you name it. However, the importance of something that Sean "Love" Combs said years ago: "to always work with an internship mindset." He built his business, which ultimately became his dynasty, by coming to work every day with the same mindset as an intern. What that meant to him was that he had the same drive and desire to succeed that he had as an intern. That was a fundamental mindset I incorporated when facing complex challenges and when the competition was steep.

When you have an internship mindset, you don't become relaxed. You never take the time to become satisfied. But, on the other hand, you don't indulge in

When you have an internship mindset, you don't become relaxed.

complacency when you achieve your goals because there is always another goal to reach. So, when I heard him speak those words, I latched on to them, and they became like a life mantra for me. They helped me question the good and the bad to determine what I was supposed to learn from every situation I faced.

I remember when I was considering leaving a federal agency for another opportunity. I had the chance to be considered for an appointment in the Obama administration. I remember going through the vetting process of the background checks and making sure everything was clear. Then, every day I would get up and run two miles. During my run, I listened to inspirational music or people of faith recounting their daily successes. Ironically, I would listen to Bishop T. D. Jakes for my inspiration, and I get to work with Bishop Jakes today. Once I could hear the trials that other people endured and the drive that kept them going, it helped me form a healthy point of view. Listening to other people's testimonies enabled my mind, body, and spirit to be open to being used in new ways for the greater good. Ultimately, it was one of the things that propelled me to become the Regional Administrator for the U.S. Small Business Administration with the Obama administration.

THE ROAD TO OPPORTUNITY

The story began many years before that. After hearing the word "Leave" at the financial institution I worked for and returning to graduate school, I had a new mindset through which I could receive new concepts and examine different aspects of a business. Even when I worked part-time at the YMCA, I tutored kids helping them to learn concepts they were struggling with relative to mathematics or English differently. I had learned to think outside the box and taught them to see things outside the box. I didn't realize the children I was tutoring were the sons and daughters of CEOs and elected officials. When I would run into these notable people, they

I had learned to think outside the box and taught them to see things outside the box.

would say, "Hey, my daughter/my son loves what you did for them. I'd like for you to come to this meeting I'm having; maybe you can be helpful."

Of course, I would reply, "Okay, great." I didn't know at the time that these people were putting me in a position to succeed. It was not something that I asked for. It was a by-product of doing something I enjoyed: working with their kids. In the meantime, I was developing new mindsets and professional practices that helped me get appointed to official boards. And when I applied for certain positions, these experiences enabled me to serve in those positions effectively. To a degree, I was springboarded into roles that I would never have considered before. The opportunity to utilize my skills and ideas with kids was a training ground for something more significant in my life.

At this point, I began to realize that the people I was introduced to recognize my passion and zeal. Because I continued to walk in humility and not arrogance, they were not afraid to take an chance on me. Moreover, they believed that giving me a chance would have

Because I continued to walk in humility and not arrogance, they were not afraid to take an chance on me.

reciprocal benefits. I could never have envisioned how working part-time at the YMCA helped me move into positions I could never have dreamed of. It led to my receiving a Presidential Management Fellowship during the George W. Bush administration. Over ten thousand people applied for that position, with four hundred accepted nationwide. I was one of those four hundred. They looked at my drive, passion, desire to be a better public administrator, and most of all, a better person—things that all persons who want to serve a municipality or large public governmental entity need to succeed.

WILLING TO BE TAUGHT

Mayor Jackson was one of those people who saw that in me. When I was in graduate school, my mentor said, "You will be in the position to do some great things, but you must be prepared to do what is right. What do you want to do with your career?"

I replied, "I want to make a difference."

"How do you plan on making a difference?"

"I believe in just giving it my all," I said.

Mayor Jackson replied, "That's pretty broad."

I agreed that my thirty-second pitch was a failure. But I recognized my mistake and persevered.

He responded, "Well, with some refining, some education, and some good experiences, you'll be able to tailor that desire into something a little more defining."

So how did I do that? I began to volunteer for campaigns, supporting people running for elected office. I worked as a volunteer in Atlanta Mayor Shirley Franklin's campaign, which Kasim Reed led. Kasim, also my fraternity brother (Kappa Alpha Psi Fraternity, Inc.), became the 59th Mayor of the city of Atlanta. His brother, Tracey Reed, was known for holding many political and business relationships together. He also helped other people achieve their goals in political office. Several of us formed a bond, which created a powerful machine. It was a good experience in my life, for it enabled me to meet many influential people, and these people gave me a great deal of wisdom.

Ultimately, those people were elected to the offices of mayor, governor, senator, congressman, and congresswoman. It wasn't just within one state; this was across the country. I didn't realize that when I was appointed as the Regional Administrator for the U.S. Small Business Administration, my background had already been checked, and people recalled all the work I had done before pursuing my government career. When I was appointed to my role, more than three hundred people applied for that role. I was fortunate to be chosen. It was ordained for me, and I sensed the presence of grace and mercy in my life.

I felt honored to be selected as that one person to be trusted to take on such a huge responsibility. I was in a stable place and surrounded myself with people who strove to be better, no matter who they were—whether cleaning the bathrooms at night or CEOs in the corner office. The federal background process was rigorous. They checked with everyone from my childhood through my professional work. I was so honored to be in a position to receive that appointment. I look back on it and realize it started with me finding my passion, following my desire to work in a place that would be conducive for my growth, and knowing that I wanted to be around people who said, "Hey, can you believe? We believe in you. You believe in yourself."

When times were dark, I could find humor and laugh at myself. When my car broke down, and it was raining, I started laughing. Taking life in its every form and fashion creates something in you that makes you realize you are in tune with life. It becomes contagious. It becomes attractive. If you want to be pulled toward something, be pulled toward your life's mission. If you can do that consistently, everything we discussed will take shape. As leaders, practitioners, and people who can give suggestions and ideas and guide them, we know we are just like you. We're receiving that wisdom from a higher place. Sometimes it's gleaned from within the community, within families, within loved ones, and with all, we learn, we prepare ourselves to be the ultimate facilitators.

Do you believe in yourself?

CHAPTER 8

YOU ARE A SUPERHERO!
WHAT'S YOUR SUPERPOWER?

Lessons from Dr. Kenneth Taylor and overcoming sleep apnea

You are a superhero. So, let's talk about being a superhero who has superpowers. What does that mean? When I think about people in our society, I realize we are such romantics that we are drawn to super beings like Superman, Batman, Wonder Woman, Green Lantern, and Black Panther. We relish these super beings, saying, "Wow, they are incredible!" What we admire about these superheroes is that they possess certain qualities that we wish we had, virtues like strength, courage, honor, and a desire to help masses of people move forward. That's what superheroes do! It is my belief, however, that we

> **We all possess a distinction that gives us a specific "super" ability.**

all are superheroes. We all possess a distinction that gives us a specific "super" ability. If you don't believe it, I do. I believe that I have a "C"

I believe that I have a "C" on my chest.

on my chest, and I believe I'm my own superhero. I believe that you are, too!

I'm sure the next question that comes to your mind is, "But what are your superpowers?" I'm glad you asked because I've got a couple of them. One of my superpowers is to focus on what most of us have, but many take it for granted: the ability to discern situations and to be intu-itive. Discernment, or intuition, is

Discernment, or intuition, is like a pot of gumbo.

like a pot of gumbo. It's a splash of intuition. It's a bit of courage and a lot of risk-taking. It is being able to make huge decisions that could ultimately put you in a place of being so vulnerable that you could be outside the mainstream instead of in.

An example is when I left my job on a whim because of my faith. It led to my doing things that I had not considered before. I forged ahead into territories new to me that opened opportunities to help masses of people. It led to engagements where I could engage audiences by speaking to them in such a way that they were both motivated and challenged to do superhero things, too.

For everyone looking to unlock their superpowers, all they need to do is look at where they've been, where they are currently, and where they ultimately want to be. Assessing what factors propelled them to their current place is essential in moving forward. What was the setting—what were the challenges that kept you up at night? Were you upset, sorrowful, or crying? What was the "need" in your life that opened your eyes and made you grab the gift of life and say, "I'm going for it"? A colleague and friend, Stephen Smith, an attorney for the federal government, once talked about his superpowers. He reminded me that his ability to put his family first in all that he does makes his life a much better place. His ability to delegate significant issues concerning how it impacts his family makes all those other things appear minor. I've borrowed some of Stephen's "superpowers" within my own walk. I think you can do the same by examining the traits of some of your friends and colleagues.

THE GIFT OF LIFE

We all have one superhero strength in common: the gift of life. No matter what your circumstances are, what you've been through, or your position in life, you still have the advantage of life. If today you're able to hear what I'm saying and read what I'm saying, you have the gift of life, and therein is a superhuman strength that needs to be tapped into. There is strength in you to do the things your heart is yearning for. Maybe you're a person who may not have been born with a silver spoon in your mouth, but you desire an education. You may not be able to pay for it or even think you are smart enough to complete the courses, but the super-power in you can accomplish it. It begins by taking the first step.

There is strength in you to do the things your heart is yearning for.

Wake up this day, take on that superhero spirit you've been given, that gift of life, and determine that you will do what needs to be done to reach your next goal. It is incumbent upon you to find out what that unique gift is that you've been given. The world is waiting for it. I have discovered and am still learning that I have more blessings than I realized.

Fight the fear that tries to hold you back. Remember, you are a superhero who can conquer any challenge you face.

Remember, you are a superhero who can conquer any challenge you face.

Over ten years ago, I volunteered my time during a campaign. Sitting in my living room after working all day, I was exhausted. As I stood up, I noticed that my heart started palpitating. I assumed I had a heart attack. I got into my car and started driving to the hospital, even with my heart racing and feeling delusional.

On the way to the hospital, I saw a college friend and asked him to drive because I didn't feel safe driving. While driving, he saw me working with my phone and asked me what I was doing. I told him that I was trying to put all my necessary information in my phone, like passwords to accounts, so that if someone needed to access my data, they could. He replied, "Dude, don't worry about that." He started laughing. That laughter calmed me down. Once again, humor intervened to change my situation.

I told him, "Dude, don't get in an accident right now because if you do, no one will hear my story. They won't know what happened. You'll be the last one." We went back and forth, making jokes. When I arrived at the hospital, I was calm.

It was good thing that I was calm, for the doctor came in and explained that I had something unique called lone atrial fibrillation, an irregular heartbeat brought on by dehydration or low potassium. In addition to the A-fib, my blood pressure was high, and he continued his diagnosis, saying that I probably had sleep apnea and would require a CPAP machine to breathe appropriately. I asked him, "So I'm not going to die?"

He said, "No, you're not going to die. But if you don't deal with it, you could have a blood clot that could get caught in your lungs, which could be catastrophic. So, we don't want that to happen."

I said, "No, we don't. What can I do?"

"Well, you need to change your lifestyle."

It goes back to my being a superhero. So I replied, "Okay, great."

EARNING MY SUPERHERO LETTER

After that day, I put on my "D" for "drive." I tried to change my lifestyle and eating habits and take the time to rest. I did the sleep study. I would have to use a CPAP machine for about four years. And during that time, I changed my eating habits. I began to get more sleep. I began to prioritize my life and realize that I am essential and must take care of myself before anyone else. In essence, I started taking care of myself. Years later, when it was time for me to retake the CPAP study, I was astonished by the results. In the end, the technician got my attention. "Mr. Cassius?"

"Yes," I said. "Is the test over?"

And he said, "Yes, you were asleep like a baby."

I said, "Well, okay. So, when do I get a new machine? Do I keep ...?"

He said, "You no longer have sleep apnea."

"What?"

"You have no traces of sleep apnea," he said.

I responded, "Wow, just adjusting little things awakened another area of my inner superhero, and I received a healing?"

In addition, being kind and complimenting people, acknowledging them for what they do, creates the kind of atmosphere that I want to live in. Also, relying on my faith—making simple changes—made my challenging times easy and helped me walk along the pathway to better health. To this day, I no longer have sleep apnea. My weight is under control. I'm not on prescription pills. My superhero strength drive kicked in and changed how I governed myself daily. I must credit my cardiologist, Dr. Kenneth Taylor, an exceptional physician, for his wisdom and friendship. Good advice and support are why I'm here today.

What letter is on your chest?

CHAPTER 9

PLANTING SEEDS AND DISCERNING HARVEST TIME

Lessons from Aubrey Branch and Dr. William Pickard

Let's talk now about planting seeds and knowing when to harvest them. I like the idea of planting seeds, but I've learned that some seeds take five, ten, or even fifteen years before they bloom. So let's talk about knowing when to harvest them! Aubrey Branch, whom I admire as a friend and big brother, often tells me to continue to plant seeds but, more importantly, know when to harvest them. Originally from New Orleans, Aubrey has built a successful insurance company in Las Vegas, Nevada, by planting business seeds. His business has flourished because of this approach.

When you're planting seeds, you must consider that there is a maturation process. The key word is **process**. For seeds to yield fruit, you must leave them in the ground and do what most people find is the hardest to do: wait! The maturation process of sowing relationship-building seeds entails giving yourself time for your connections to develop so that they can build on each other for something unique to emerge. Your seed might produce an idea, access to new opportunities, or a collaboration. But it may not happen overnight. Give yourself time for your relationship seeds to take root.

The road to being exceptional is easier to travel with friends. Learn to plant seeds among the people you meet, and then know when it's time to harvest. Make it your business to adopt a lifestyle of planting seeds of relationship building, and when it's time to harvest, you'll reap the benefits of having a wide network of connections that prove to be your most valuable assets.

Adopt a lifestyle of planting seeds of relationship building.

I have been fortunate to have a small group of special friends to support my journey since my late teenage years. We call ourselves, The Ravens. That term "Ravens" came from a sermon given by Dr. Otis Moss III years ago. It basically talked about "ravens" the bird itself known for very seldom seen alone. Ravens typically are in a group, in all aspects of their daily walk or light. Catherine Jefferson, Roger Morales, M.D., Melissa Fields, Mario Tukes, Melodye Tukes, Jesse Bacon, Esq., Victor Washington, and Anthony Lacy are members of The Ravens. Each year we take a cabin retreat to discuss our future, debate our challenges, replenish our spirits, and acknowledge our growth. I would encourage you to explore a group of individuals you can trust and rely on personally and professionally.

As human beings, we all need each other at various times. You are networking when you progress through life, planting seeds of goodwill. You are networking with people that you may be familiar with or unfamiliar with. You may be networking or engaging in relationships with people with whom you have something in common, or you may need their professional help. It may even be someone who will be significant in your personal life, and you don't realize that at the time. Whatever the case, there is one thing that can serve you as a qualifier: you have something to offer, too. As you begin planting seeds in other people's gardens, realize that you are also cultivating opportunities you may need for the future.

Therefore, when planting, offer some fertilization and some sunshine. Even offer water to dry soil. Plant near already-established trees so your seed will someday provide shade for the weary traveler. When the plants begin to grow, you will find that the seeds you planted in other people's gardens will flourish and that someone has planted seeds in your garden as well, and they are growing.

REAPING THE HARVEST

Pollination and seed dispersal is critical to the survival of plant species. When a flower blooms, it gives off specific chemicals or possesses certain components that attract pollinators, such as bees and butterflies. The pollinators spread the pollen, enabling the flowers to ripen into seed-bearing fruit. The seeds are then dispersed, or distributed, by wind, water, or animals. Animals depend on the energy from the nectar or the fruit; plants depend on animals to provide mobility. Everything is connected. Think about that in relation to human relationships: when you plant seeds, you initiate relationships. You begin to grow ideas. You begin to product concepts people can use at some point. When and how they use these concepts is

Be the exception by planting the seeds and trusting the process.

not for you to determine. You can't be selfish or impatient and think you will see the harvest. Be the exception by planting the seeds and trusting the process.

People often do not realize that this is networking—going to places where you may be uncomfortable and fostering relationships. Recently, I was at my dear alma mater, Morehouse College. I was so glad to go back and speak at the Department of Business & Economics, where I serve as an advisor. I had a chance to talk about opportunities for acquiring funding for business-related projects. The school's leadership wanted me to talk about business, as it applied to seniors aspiring to work in that field. It was exciting and right up my lane.

When I arrived to speak to the class, I brought a good friend named of Dr. Kevin Woods, another Morehouse alum. Kevin is an accomplished physician and the president of the Atlanta Medical Association. He is just as astute as an entrepreneur as he is in medicine.

The professor opened the discussion with introductions. Next, we engaged in a group discussion, which was very enlightening. We were supposed to be there an hour and 45 minutes. Instead, we talked for three hours! The debate became contagious. We were invited to another class to come in and continue the conversation. We realized that we were given opportunities to minds that wanted to learn how to succeed in business and life.

We talked about planting seeds. I didn't come to speak to get an honorarium. I am aware that other experts in the field can deliver a message better than I can. Yet, because they asked me, I gave it all the passion I could and shared valuable experiences. As a result, when I was leaving, I was asked to come back again the next month to talk to two other classes. That is an example of why I plant seeds and use intuition to discern when it's harvest time. There is a joy that comes with the fruit of your labor.

One way of looking at harvesting seeds too soon is to think about a banana when it is green. You can't eat a green banana; you must wait until it is yellow. It's like that with relationships too. Some relationships need time to mature, but never view a relationship as unimportant.

Never view a relationship as unimportant.

Dr. Pickard is another mentor who often discusses the importance of relationships in your business and personal brand. Dr. William "Bill" Pickard is the chairman of ARD Logistics and part owner of the MGM Grand Hotel – in Detroit, Michigan. He serves on several national boards and credits his success to having genuine, dependable relationships that started with planted seeds. Mentors and friends like Dr. Pickard have helped me recognize the difference between seed time and harvest and how to appreciate both in business and in life.

What seeds of relationships can you start planting or nurturing today?

CHAPTER 10

YOU ARE MORE POWERFUL
THAN YOU THINK

Lessons from being honored by the Atlanta Business League

When you think of what it takes to be successful, you must imagine your success and see yourself at the finish line. Prepare for the final goal before starting your journey. Remember that people see your gifts and abilities as you have packaged them. When I think of the experiences that have prepared me for personal and professional success, it hinges on my decision to remain humble. That aura of humility is a gift I walk in and never take for granted. Even when I do my best work and receive accolades, I still remember the roads I have taken that brought me to this place.

Thus, no matter how many goals I may attempt to achieve, it all goes back to me walking in faith, trusting God for the results, and maintaining a sense of humility. These factors are more

It all goes back to me walking in faith, trusting God for the results, and maintaining a sense of humility.

powerful than all my planning and preparation. And the marvelous thing is that each of us possesses the same opportunity to walk in these qualities. We can all possess the same mindset of faith and humility that will ignite our passion into a fire that will burn for us.

MY VIEW OF SUCCESS

I was fortunate enough to receive an award from the Atlanta Business League. The Atlanta Business League is one of the country's oldest business organizations that supports people of color. Only some champions have been awarded this honor. Even though I have received other awards, this award was something special to me. The League prepared a video that addressed my accomplishments and the lives I have been affecting. I found it hard to believe that I had touched so many lives. Think about the things you have accomplished and the lives you have affected.

At the ceremony, they asked me to speak about the things that helped me attain my success. I told them I would not only thank everyone in the room but also inform them that I would speak about what motivated me and where my power is derived. I wanted the illustrious company to present at this occasion to know who and what makes me what I am. Here is an excerpt of what I said that day:

> *"I'm grateful to have met a senator from Illinois in 2007 who later became the president of the United States. He heard my selfless story of wanting to make a difference. He allowed me the opportunity to carry out those wishes and make certain that communities, families, and businesses had the opportunity to live their entrepreneurial dreams. In addition, I would like to recognize my mother and brother, who instilled the faith that governs me daily. People often ask me, 'What will you do next after the Obama administration is over?' I often smile and say, 'The same thing I was doing before I had this role. God's will.'*
>
> *When you see me lead, I hope you think of Moses, a sinner-turned-general leading God's people from despair to freedom. When you hear me speaking and*

spending more time with servants than CEOs, I hope you are reminded of Solomon's ability to seek wisdom from every walk of life. And when you observe me spinning and thanking those around me, I hope you think of David, trying to win the hearts of many, only to acknowledge that life is more significant than any one person. I came into this world with a stamp on my chest called favor. And what you may not see (but always there) are grace and mercy, standing to the left and right of me, which are my protectors."

I finished by saying, *"Thank you, Atlanta Business League, and thank you for your time and attention. Stay encouraged."*

When I walked off that stage, the person behind me said, "Wow, I think that's the end of the show. That's it." The truth is, my speech wasn't about me getting any praise or recognition; rather, I wanted the recognition to go to the One who has helped me throughout my life. I recognize where my strength comes from, and I wanted everyone to know that I realized now that

I wanted the recognition to go to the One who has helped me throughout my life.

I was much stronger than my teenage self could have imagined. I also recognize that even with the strength that resides within me, there are still mountains to climb. Most of all, I wanted the audience to know that the same strength lay in each of them. I will continue to give that power and strength away for the rest of my life. It is what fulfills me.

Is there a time in your life when you saw a substantial rise in yourself that you could use to influence others?

CHAPTER 11

DISRUPTORS ARE NECESSARY

Lessons from Governor Brian Kemp,
Ambassador Andrew Young and Melissa Wikoff

Let's talk about disruptors. Disruptors are not necessarily haters; disruptors are those people, groups, or individuals that will try to take you off your path of success. They are those people who will challenge you and engage you in a way that is unlike your usual way of governing yourself. They will get you to take your eyes off the prize. They are those groups or individuals that will put you in a place where you begin to have self-doubt and rethink how you will achieve your dreams. Despite this description, disruptors are necessary.

Disruptors sometimes cause conflict. I welcome conflict. I look for conflict; I engage in conflict because, as one comedian said, "That means if I have one more "hater" by the end of summer, I know that I'm getting closer to my dream." So, I see those people trying to take me off my path and challenge me as nec-

"If I have one more 'hater' by the end of summer, I know that I'm getting closer to my dream."

essary for my development. The enemy will reveal itself once you're close to your goal. The enemy may not necessarily be some person walking around with pointy ears and a pitchfork, but they'll show up as negative people with negative vibes who are not happy to see you succeed because they are having challenges within themselves.

Sometimes it is personal insecurity that makes people try to tear you down. Whether continuing your education or closing a business deal, disruptors will be in the middle of that. Expect disruption and learn to identify where it is coming from. I now look at disruptors and laugh! I look at them and say, "I see you; I identify who you are. No, you cannot have what I have. Yes, I will achieve my dreams, and you can't stop me!"

When you acknowledge your disruptors, they may say, "Hey, I didn't realize I was doing that to you. I didn't realize

I hurt your feelings. I didn't realize I was trying to throw you off your path." That is, if they are genuine. But sometimes, people are intentionally disruptive. It pays to be aware that, no matter what, disruptors will show up, and whatever path you're on, there's going to be someone or something that's going to be in direct contrast with where you're going. But, that's okay. These distractors are necessary. Don't let their *distraction* be a *detraction*. Distractions only warrant the slightest bit of attention just long enough to recognize them so you can put them in their place. However, if you spend too much time and attention on negativity and disruption, they can detract you or knock you off your game, causing you to lose focus.

Always keep haters in their place. Keep your mind on your goals and stay the course with extreme focus, realizing that there's a lesson

Always keep haters in their place.

that others can learn from watching you be the exception. That means when they watch you rise despite their attempt to throw you off, you give them the exceptionally valuable life skills of knowing who you are and standing your ground that can help them be better in their next place.

I have been fortunate to advise the likes of Georgia Governor Brian Kemp, receive counsel from Ambassador Andrew Young, and take guidance from my audiologist, Melissa Wikoff, who started her practice after learning that her grandfather suffered hearing loss from serving in WWII. She taught me how to manage my condition of tinnitus. They have chosen to follow what they believe are their passions in the hopes that they might make a positive contribution to society. We may not always agree on every topic or understand the walk of people who follow true to their profession. I like to think of it this way: If we want someone to respect our decisions, we must first respect their choices.

If we want someone to respect our decisions, we must first respect their choices.

MAKING DISRUPTORS YOUR FRIENDS

There are many ways to spread your light and share the factors that lead to your success with others. One is by including them on your path, not necessarily in a personal relationship, but by allowing them to view you while you demonstrate your success. For example, I often invite close friends and family to participate in my speaking engagements so they can hear how I address others and give me a critique regarding how I can do better.

I remember my first week on the job when I served in the federal government. A hurricane had hit the entire Southeast. It was a catastrophic storm involving a tornado, and the hurricane destroyed many small businesses and homes. I was sent there to talk to the small businesses, get them back on their feet and inform them of products we had that could help their professional community. When I arrived, there were news cameras, and many people were sitting around. There were some people placing sandbags down to stop the flow of water. I remember getting out of the car and a guy walking up to me to saying, "Hey, I'm looking for the regional administrator for SBA. When's he getting here?"

"I think he's here now," I said.

Then he said, "I need you to help me with these bags." He didn't realize he was looking for me.

So, I helped to put down sandbags and these huge blocks. I also helped assemble signs showing people where to go for help. People whose businesses had been closed because of the storms were there to get fast loans to pay their employees. Yet here I was, helping them put up this temporary space so people could line up to get assistance. After about an hour, my communications director said, "Hey, they're looking for the regional administrator." And she started laughing. One of the people asked why she was laughing, and she replied, "That's him."

He said, "Who? This guy right here?"

She said, "Yeah, the same guy who's been helping you for the last hour. It's him." And we all laughed.

I point out that the people who did not recognize me were not doing it to be mean or hurtful; they just assumed it couldn't be me. I didn't have a suit and tie on. I came ready to work, and that threw some people off. I may have looked at them like a disruptor. People tend to assume the worst instead of the best. I welcome that, and because that is who I am and my approach to what I do, we were able to come to common ground and realize that we were all part of the same team. We were all there to help the community get back on its feet, so we put our titles aside to be of service to others.

That was one example of how to be the exception when a potential disruptor comes on the scene. People may not have intended to hurt you or be malicious or mean. They don't always know your status. If I had been prideful with my new position, and gotten offended, I would have missed the opportunity to leave a positive, lasting impression. Through staying humble, yet knowing who I am, I was able to show people how to respond when people underestimate or make assumptions about you. Always remember that people can assume the worst no matter who you are, how well your appearance is, or what your background may be. I like to **give them my best and let them make up their minds in the end.**

If I had been prideful and gotten offended, I would have missed the opportunity to leave a positive, lasting impression.

Think about the last time you encountered a disruptor or hater. What did you do in the moment? How will you be the exception to the rule the next time a disruptor comes along?

CHAPTER 12

THIS IS MY DECK OF CARDS; NOW WHAT?

Lessons from Sam Olens and playing the hand you are dealt

Think about what you want to do with what you have. You get this deck of cards and say to yourself, "How am I going to play this out? How am I going to win? How am I going to come out on top of this?" I consider myself the UNO king. I used to love to play UNO, even though I never played the other card games that often. When you're dealt your hand, you assess your cards and consider what you can do with them. I would take pride in remembering the colors and the numbers simultaneously. It would give me a clear advantage when deciding what card to play. With card games, you must take chances, even though you can only play with the cards you've been dealt. Sometimes you can turn all your cards in and build another deck, hoping for a better hand. I believe in creating my own deck, atmosphere, and the essence of who I truly am. This model inspires other people to do the same thing.

Although you may have a less-than-perfect hand, use that as a basis to stand on, build upon, and get to the next place you want to be. Some time ago, there was a regional leadership institute program. This program would help aspiring planners or professionals looking to work in the federal government or local municipalities. It helped train prospective employees for their next level of professional work. The clients served were typically appointed by politicians. I applied for this opportunity, and after researching it, I knew it was something I needed.

Although you may have a less-than-perfect hand, use that as a basis to stand on and build upon.

THE EXCEPTION TO THE RULE

There was an elected official in the state of Georgia named Sam Olens. Today, he is an accomplished attorney with a global law firm. At that time, Sam was influential in the political arena and was and still is revered by his peers and community. I had a chance to meet him when I was completing my graduate program. "Cassius," he said, "I see you were accepted into the regional leadership institute. You have an amazing story. We, as elected officials, normally appoint people to be a part of this. So how did you get in?" I thought to myself: what a privilege to be a part of such an esteemed group. Business leaders and elected officials in my class had already accomplished many achievements.

"Well, sir," I said, "I just saw it. I saw the people who were in it previously. I knew this was the area I wanted to be in, and I just applied. And I didn't have anyone to sponsor me; I just did it."

He replied, "You're an exception to anyone I've seen, but I think you have a promising future."

At this meeting, I began to recognize that **there is a mindset called being an exception to the rule.** For at this regional institute, I was an exception to the rule that was in place. I realized I had a deck of cards that

Being an exception to the rule... it's a mindset!

was different from who I was supposed to be and what I was supposed to do in life. I had my unique deck and could play it out for my benefit. I might have impressed Sam so much that I was later recommended and appointed to the Workforce Development Board in Cobb County. I served on that board for seven years. I realized I didn't need a specific hand to play cards; I could play the hand I was dealt and make it work for me. I could make up my rules if they stayed within legal, moral, and professional boundaries. Other than that, the game was mine to win!

The concept of "This is your deck of cards; now what?" allows you as an individual to create the rule that is best for you. You realize that you are a beacon of light that can shine, no matter how you start. I want to return to the fact that people are attracted

You are a beacon of light that can shine, no matter how you start.

to how you do things when you walk in humility. It doesn't matter what deck of cards you start with; it matters how you play them to achieve a winning end.

Now, what are you going to do with your deck of cards?

CHAPTER 13

YOU ARE AS UNIQUE AS A SNOWFLAKE—EMBRACE IT

Lessons from being underestimated, corporate America, and customer service

I was born in West Philadelphia but finished high school in Orlando, Florida. During my formative years, I was exposed to two different places with different living styles. In Philly, the winters were cold and rainy. In Orlando, it never got cold! But I did enjoy them both. Whether it was a snowflake or a hurricane, the uniqueness of both environments could create a trial. Storms, too, are unique. They are powerful and memorable enough to be given names like Katrina or Henry.

> **Whether it was a snowflake or a hurricane, the uniqueness of both environments could create a trial.**

Everyone is unique in their own way. They are also unique in the way they become superheroes. We all have different powers and abilities. And being unique and different from other people is something that takes time to embrace. But embracing your extraordinary true self will mean that no matter what you think, what you want to be in life, or who you think you want to be like, you are the only person in the entire world who can be YOU. We begin to mature when we embrace our unique selves. Doing so will enable you to make your EXCEPTIONAL contribution to society.

You are the only person in the entire world who can be YOU.

Once you realize that you are your unique self, you will then embrace the fact that no one can replicate what you do. You will then realize that you have a distinct purpose, and that purpose has the power to influence others. You can take your passion out of the box and let it take you to that place of purpose.

MAKING IT WORK FOR YOU

I remember going through the development program at a national financial institution. I looked younger than I was at the time. It took a long time for me to grow facial hair! At the time, a customer walked into the banking center when I was conducting a training session. He said, "I want to talk to the branch manager right now. I'm having a problem with my account."

I said, "Okay. Yes, sir. How may I help you?"

"No, excuse me," he replied. "I don't need to talk to you. You're too wet behind the ears. I need to talk to the branch manager to help me resolve this situation."

"Well, I can help you."

"Listen, young fellow. I want to talk to the person in charge."

"Well, sir, I'm happy to tell you that as odd as it may seem, I'm that person in charge here today, and I'm here to help you with your account."

And he looked at me, confused.

"That can't possibly be you. You're too young. You don't have enough miles on your sneakers. It can't be you."

"No, it is actually me," I said. "Let's go to my office and see how I can help you." So we talked through his situation and worked it out. I also brought in other specialists who could help him, his wife, and his family set up three different accounts that day without him having to come up with money out of his pocket.

When we left, I walked him to the door and offered him my hand for a shake. Then, I said, "Well, thank you for coming in today."

"Actually," he replied, "thank you. You taught me a valuable lesson. As you mentioned before, you are unique. That's going to go a long way in your career, sonny."

"Well, thank you very much, sir," I said. "Thank you very much for coming in today." I realized then that my baby face, while unique, did not inhibit what I had to offer.

And that is what we're getting to. You can be unique, but that doesn't take away the fact that you have something to offer in your uniqueness. You possess something that can help people. It is often not a unique skill; sometimes, it is simple, like being kind to someone who particularly needs it that day. It can be as simple as utilizing your relationships to help someone get ahead or offering that

You have something to offer in your uniqueness.

person who needs financial assistance. You may not be able to give them money out of your pocket, but you can direct them to resources you are familiar with. By being who I am, I offer unique characteristics that can help someone. My greatest desire is to be just me—the man God created me to be.

Now ask yourself this question: Who were you created to be?

CHAPTER 14

BE FAIR, COMPLIMENT OFTEN, BUT DON'T EXPECT THE SAME IN RETURN

Lessons from Dr. Louis Lynn

This is a crucial chapter. First, I want to introduce a concept that is often difficult for people to implement. It is challenging because most people feel if they do something for someone else, that person should also do something for them. This belief can play out in so many areas. The one I want to address, however, is recognition.

There have been many instances where I thought I deserved recognition, that it was the appropriate time to receive a compliment or an accolade. Not receiving it when I thought I should have sent me into a time of introspection. I finally got the message in my head that it was not about me getting credit; it was about getting the job done. And something more— it was about acknowledging those who helped me get the job done, personally and professionally.

It was not about me getting credit; it was about getting the job done.

THE EXCEPTIONAL ALWAYS LEAD BY GIVING

I began to realize that I needed to be fair to everyone on a project, and instead of looking for a compliment, I gave a compliment. One of the people who refined that way of thinking for me is Dr. Louis Lynn. Dr. Lynn is the founder of a family-owned business and a member of Clemson University's board of trustees. In addition, he serves on the Atlanta Advisory Board for Truist Bank and the National Urban League. He is the quintessential example of a good family man and a successful executive. I am proud to call him my mentor.

Instead of looking for a compliment, I gave a compliment.

Recently, there was an excellent opportunity at Georgia State University, where I served as an executive in residence.

The faculty needed a speaker to be present for a huge event that was taking place, but they needed help acquiring one because of scheduling conflicts. I offered to help reach out to the proposed speaker while working with a contract planner for the event. I informed the potential speaker, "I need you to speak at this event. It'll be a huge favor for me, and I think it's something that is going be beneficial for the university and us as well." I credit my good friend T. Dallas Smith for taking the liberty of helping me to join the GSU School of Business family. He had previously served as a trustee.

I saw the event planning through the entire process, and the day of the event came and went. For some reason, I wasn't invited to the event. I later ran into the speaker one day and said, "Hello. Great speech?"

He said, "Where were you? You asked me to be there. We delivered a great speech. Everyone was there. Where were you?"

Instead of telling him I wasn't invited, I said, "Well, there was a conflict, and I was unable to attend."

"You know what? I acknowledged you during the speech. I wanted you to know I was there because you asked me to be there."

I felt strange about the whole event when I realized I had not been invited and wanted to say how I thought it was unfair for me not to be present. Instead, when there was another event with another great speaker, I invited those individuals who did not ask me to attend the event at Georgia State. I arranged for them to be involved in the event and gave them seats front and center. I also saw to it that they were acknowledged for the work that they had done because it was the right thing to do. I didn't expect anything in return for this effort. I did it because that's what I would want to be done for me. I later discovered that my non-invitation to Georgia State had been a misunderstanding. They had just assumed that I would be present. I had exercised my humility and not asked to come, so I didn't realize this.

Knowing that you're going to go through life where people are not always going to acknowledge or praise you for a job well done can be a bitter pill to swallow. People aren't always going to give you your accolades. There could be a variety of reasons. They may have forgotten or been dealing with personal things that prevented them from acknowledging and complimenting you.

People aren't always going to give you your accolades.

Whatever the reason, what I know is that if you want to receive fair treatment, if you want to be complimented, if you want to be recognized, then you must first give those things. You must maintain an attitude of making a fair assessment of others without pre-judging them. It would be best to acknowledge people, whether they recognize you or not, because people work harder than you can imagine. They deserve that. You must know that it is the right thing to do.

You must maintain an attitude of making a fair assessment of others without pre-judging them.

Doing the right thing ignites your passion. And remember, if you follow your passion, you'll never get lost. If you're honest, sometimes you may receive unfair treatment, but I guarantee that if you put more energy into being fair and complimentary, rewards will come back to you when you need them. Don't expect to know how it will happen or who will return them. Decide to be consistent, to be fair, to be direct, and to be generous in acknowledging someone when it's their time.

###

These are my thoughts on being exceptional in the things you think, say, and do. My ask to you now is that you take these thoughts as the clues to success that they are intended to be, and use them as a compass to guide you on your journey to becoming EXCEPTIONAL.

Here's to being the exception to the rule!

TO BE CONTINUED...

MORE FROM THE AUTHOR

Want to connect and network with me and other people who dare to be the exception to the rule?

Your journey to being exceptional doesn't have to end with this book. Join the **Exception-aires Community** where you can connect with a group of likeminded people who are finding their passion, living their purpose and doing amazing things in their work and in their communities. Learn more here:

You belong here!

Scan the QR Code
or visit
CassiusButts.com/exceptions

Connect with me online: www.CassiusButts.com

in Cassius F. Butts   cassiusfbutts   f Cassius Butts

Media and speaking inquiries:
CassiusButts.com/speaking